SOUTH FOR SUNSHINE

Tony Hillman and Beverley Cole

Capital Transport

First published 1999

ISBN 185414 213 5

Published in association with the
National Railway Museum by
Capital Transport Publishing,
38 Long Elmes, Harrow Weald,
Middlesex

Printed by CS Graphics, Singapore

Most of the posters in this book are from the collection of
the National Railway Museum, and the publicity items from
the collection of Tony Hillman. We are also grateful to Aldo
Delicato and Stan Friedman for other items.

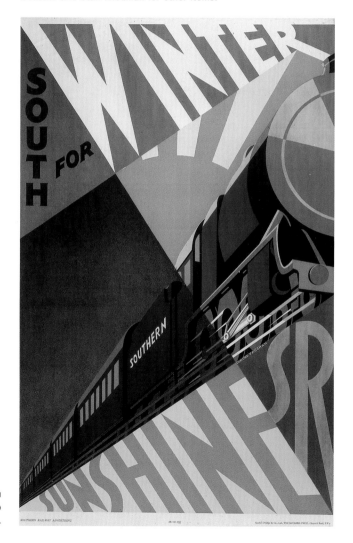

South for Winter Sunshine by Edmond Vaughan
A steam loco hauled train is used to good effect with art deco
colouring and lettering in this 1929 poster.

A handbill advertising the train service for the Southern Railway's first Easter service. The style of logo, with the initials of the three main pre-grouping companies, was used immediately after the grouping.

'Hints for Holidays' was the longest running publication. Started by the London and South Western Railway in 1899, it was continued by the Southern Railway with the final edition produced by British Railways in 1949. The 1924 edition was produced in sections each with an attractive cover depicting a scene from the area covered.

Introduction

When the Southern Railway came into existence at the railway grouping on January 1 1923 it took over a very active publicity machine. The three main companies that were formed into the Southern Railway had produced many guidebooks and posters attempting to persuade customers to use their railways. The London and South Western Railway, which covered the large holiday areas from Hampshire to North Devon and Cornwall, was the most prolific. The South Eastern and Chatham, in South East England, and the London Brighton and South Coast Railway, whose area fitted between the other two, also had much publicity covering their parts of Southern England.

The origins of railway publicity, however, go back further than that produced by the pre-grouping companies. As early as 1839 a booklet was published by James Wild called *The London and Southampton Railway Guide*. Later, the publishers and the railway companies joined forces and guidebooks were published with the railway companies' approval, the words 'Printed by Authority' being found on the cover or title page to denote this agreement. The London and South Western Railway was one of the first to produce its own guidebooks in the early 1890s.

The London and South Western Railway Publicity Department was created in 1913 by the General Manager Sir Herbert Walker as a section of the General Manager's Office. This brought together all the advertising and publicity activities previously spread around various departments.

It was from this base that the Southern Railway publicity machine grew and it is hoped that this small book will serve as a useful guide to the company's publicity art.

Very few Southern Railway publications covered topics that had not previously been included in a pre-grouping title. All three companies produced guidebooks to the areas they served and to areas further afield which could be reached via their railway. Brittany was well represented, as was the north of France and Belgium. Attempts were also made to increase use of the railway for leisure activities such as rambling or golf by the production of guidebooks covering these areas.

With all this material at its disposal the Southern Railway took some time to sort out what it was keeping and what it was merging with other publicity. There was much duplication of areas covered by two guidebooks from different pre-grouping companies. As the Southern Railway publicity department was housed at Waterloo, and in the main staffed by ex-London and South Western employees, there seems to have been a bias to expand the London and South Western Railway titles to

South for Sunshine Holidays by Southern Railway
The cover of this 1926 leaflet shows the most well
known image that was used by the Southern
Railway. The child is Ronald Witt and his father
took the photograph. They were emigrating to
Canada and Ronald was talking to the fireman of
the train taking them from Waterloo to
Southampton. Ronald's father, a former employee
of the Southern Railway, provided a copy of the
photograph to the railway in case it could be used
in the Southern Railway's house magazine. The
potential of the photograph was immediately
realised and from 1925 it appeared in posters all
over the Southern Railway system and was
reproduced in national advertisements and
magazines. The factual content of the leaflet is very
similar to that produced later. Holidays in Southern
England provide all that anyone could require.
Unusually some of the paragraphs have rhyming
titles, such as 'Sunny Shores and Cooling Breezes,
Southern Coastline always pleases', and 'The Sun
shines most on the Southern Coast'.

There is Sunshine in the South by P. Irwin Brown, 1930.
Here the message is conveyed by the strength of colour and simplicity of design. No doubt the development of printing processes and colour printing helped this. The lettering is also very modern and angularly futuristic.

Here the Railway system is symbolic of speed and change: the rapid transportation to sunshine. The train is the means of carrying the traveller away from the dark, cold city into a green, warm countryside.

include the other constituents rather than the other way around. For up to three years the Southern Railway continued with some of the old titles with virtually no change other than the replacement of the old company name with Southern Railway and the appropriate division, for example Southern Railway (Eastern Division).

Though the new Southern Railway was investing heavily on electrification and new rolling stock the changes brought delays and cancellations. The travelling public was not happy about this and the press strongly criticised the Southern on their behalf. At the same time London Transport was having similar problems but not getting nearly such bad public and press reaction. Lord Ashfield, founder of London Transport, suggested to Sir Herbert Walker, now the General Manager of the Southern Railway, that if the Southern Railway kept its passengers informed about what was happening not so many complaints would be forthcoming. So, in January 1925 Sir Herbert Walker decided to employ John Elliot, who previously worked on the London Evening Standard to handle the press. He became the Southern Railway's head of Public Relations and Advertising.

After his initial work providing the press with information about the efforts the Southern Railway was making to improve the situation he turned his attention to a direct approach to the commuters. He recruited E. P. Leigh-Bennett, a journalist with the *Bystander* magazine, to produce a quarterly magazine for commuters. Later, E. P. Leigh-Bennett produced many books for the Southern Railway.

Following these successes he turned his attention to posters, which he considered second-rate. Admitting he knew nothing about posters he turned to two experts whose posters were nationally known. Frank Pick was commissioning posters for London Transport and William Teasdale for the London and North Eastern Railway. One of the first series of posters produced by John Elliot was by Ethelbert White with the titles *Live in Kent and Be Content* and *Live in Surrey, Free from Worry*. From these beginnings the Southern Railway produced many hundreds of posters, the most famous being the little boy standing at the end of Waterloo station looking up at the locomotive fireman. The poster simply reads 'For holidays I always go Southern 'cos it's the Sunshine Line'.

The Southern Railway continued producing many hundreds of guidebooks to encourage travel for every conceivable reason. Books detailing all the holiday areas covered by the Southern Railway, and the near Continent that could be reached by its ships, continued on an annual basis. There were also books about boarding schools, homes in outer London, golf courses, campsites and rambling; in fact anything which encouraged people to travel. Later, as travel facilities allowed, the Southern Railway expanded its coverage to include areas previously ignored; the South of France, Spain, Italy, Greece and even Egypt.

Sunny South Sam

The face of Sunny South Sam appeared on much publicity in the early 1930s. The Southern Railway wanted to assure travellers that there was always a helpful person to assist them on their journey. The numerous Sunny South Sams were Guards who, as well as assisting travellers, could give them information about the resorts they were travelling to.

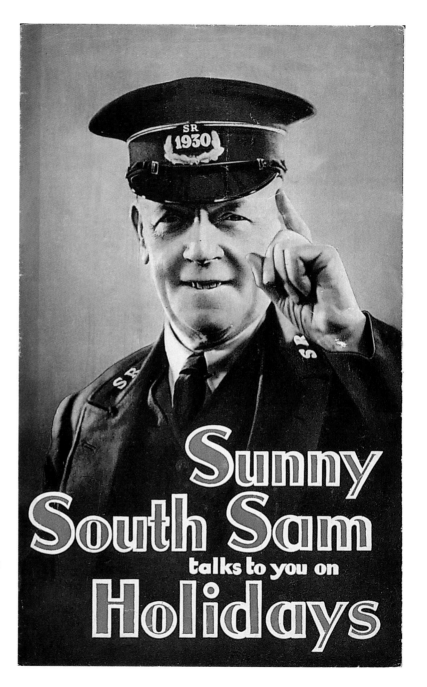

You, and me, and Holidays.

Ladies and Gentlemen,

I'm just one of the hundreds of S.R. Guards who look after you at holiday (and other) times, and I've a pretty good knowledge of the resorts the S.R. serves. So I've taken on the job of telling you what I know—where to go, how to go, quickly and cheaply and comfortably. I'm no great shakes at literature, but what I write is sincere, and I hope it will help you to have a better holiday this year than ever.

Yours faithfully,

Sunny South Sam

I have brought people back from most of the holiday-places on the Southern Railway, and I can't help noticing how they all seem to have enjoyed themselves!

If you were to ask me where you should go in the Sunny South for a holiday, I should say: " Get the Southern Railway's book 'Hints for Holidays,' " which you can buy for a tanner at any of our bookstalls or stations, and choose the place you like the look of best. With " Hints for Holidays " in your hand you will have all the information about all the holiday places in the South and South-West of England and the Channel Isles, and you can choose anywhere, from the happy crowds on the sands at Margate to some little fishing village or a quiet farmhouse among the country lanes down in the West. It all depends on the kind of holiday you want and what your circumstances are. Now as for me—well this is not the place for personal opinions, so I'll leave you to guess where I shall be going!

There are lots of seaside places of all sorts within 90 minutes' run of London. Fares don't run away with so much money if you go to one of these. On the other hand, if you want to go farther afield, you have just as big a variety of places to choose from ; and, if you have to consider the cash — as most of us do these days — there are cheap tickets that bring anywhere on the Southern within reach of anybody who takes holidays at all.

The Southern Railway is making a lot more improvements in its services this year, you know. There are going to be more restaurant cars, more long-distance expresses, and a lot more new corridor trains in which you can book your seats. Seat reservation is what the public likes, and quite right too ! You can book a seat through the Station Master for a bob any time up to 4 o'clock on the day before you travel. Then there's a good meal ready on the restaurant car (at a moderate price, too), and if a party of you are travelling, I should reserve a compartment — it keeps the party together, and only costs 5s., whether you are travelling with ordinary, tourist, week - end or long period excursion tickets.

If you'll take my tip, you'll send your luggage in advance — you can do so by simply asking for a form at any station or enquiry office—and you'll have absolutely nothing to worry about on your journey. Of course, you'll get your ticket in advance. There's no need for anybody to stand in a queue if they will only take advantage of the facilities our company offers.

Many people like to decide their holidays with an eye to their particular sport or other form of enjoyment, and there again " Hints for Holidays " will help. It tells you all about sport at whatever place you want to visit.

Finally, wherever you go, whatever you do, please remember that all of us on the Southern Railway will do our best to help you and get you there and back again comfortably and quickly.

Many small booklets and pamphlets were supposedly produced by Sam explaining facilities available to passengers. Sam wrote his booklets in a different way to other Southern Railway publicity. The introduction to his 1930 offering titled 'Sunny South Sam talks to you on Holidays' includes the phrase 'I'm no great shakes at literature, but what I write is sincere'. It is clear from the rest of the text that the Southern Railway felt that there were many potential passengers who would feel more at home with Sam's down to earth style. Sam always used colloquialisms whenever he could, for example, telling his readers to buy 'Hints for Holidays' for a *tanner* rather than the 6d used in other publicity.

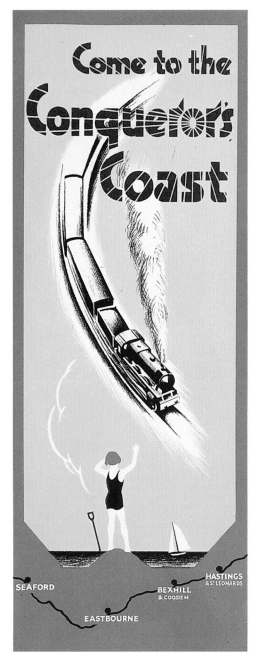

Come to the Conqueror's Coast

The Southern Railway tried to enhance the interest of areas of Southern England by using appropriate names when describing these in its publicity. Such an area was the Conqueror's Coast, between Seaford and Hastings. The leaflet illustrated suggests inside that readers should 'Come and spend a holiday on these golden shores on which the Norman Conqueror landed. Nearly a thousand years ago this glorious country lay beneath the iron heel of the invader. Today it is one of the loveliest holiday districts throughout the whole length and breadth of England. Glorious sands, mighty cliffs, backed by a countryside of surpassing loveliness, go to make up a holiday district that you will never forget.'

COME TO THE CONQUEROR'S COAST

COME and spend a holiday on these golden shores on which the Norman Conqueror landed. Nearly a thousand years ago this glorious country lay beneath the iron heel of the invader. To-day it is one of the loveliest holiday districts throughout the whole length and breadth of England. Glorious sands, mighty cliffs, backed by a countryside of surpassing loveliness, go to make up a holiday district that you will never forget.

Apart from all the natural beauty of the Conqueror's coast, there is everything that a holiday-maker can wish for—perfect bathing, quiet beaches and secluded nooks, amusements of every kind, magnificent golf courses, every facility for tennis and the best of boating and fishing. There are concert parties at the great centres, entertainments galore, dance halls, bands, and everything to make every hour of your holiday days and nights a time of sheer delight, and healthful rest and recreation.

The four great centres within East Sussex offer every variety of holiday, every kind of accommodation. There are magnificent, luxurious hotels, jolly boarding houses and quiet apartments—something to suit everybody and everbody's purse—and it all lies within ninety minutes or so of town ; so that fares do not become a heavy item of holiday expenditure.

The district is as rich in memorials of our country's historic past as it is in sylvan and coastal beauty. There are ancient castles to be visited and places which are as lovely as they are historic ; there is the whole wide expanse of the South Downs, where the Channel breezes bring you health and strength as you tread the springy turf upon their slopes.

Come to the Conqueror's coast this year and learn by experience what a jolly time you can have there. Old or young, rich or poor, there is something for everybody, and, over all, there is the glorious sunshine of the Sunny South renewing your health and energy, painting roses on the cheeks of the little ones, and tanning the faces of the grown-ups with that healthy holiday tan which is so characteristic of all those who spend a holiday upon the Conqueror's coast.

Bexhill-on-Sea by Ronald Lampitt, 1947. Bexhill was 62 miles from London and could be reached from Victoria to Bexhill Central by electric train. It sought to attract long stay holiday folk rather than trippers. It was a comparatively new town with no factories and its main industries were education (it was recognised as being one of the finest scholastic centres in the south of England) and tourism. The sea front covered six miles with a golf course at each end.

The Pavilion, opened in 1935, was named after the mayor at the time, Earl De La Warr, and housed a bathing pool, restaurant, sun lounges and a Concert Hall with a seating capacity of over 1,300. It was designed by the German architect Erich Mendelsohn, a refugee from Hitler's Germany. It is famous for its great spiral south stairs and cantilevered north staircase.

Eastbourne by Kenneth Shoesmith, 1938.
Eastbourne was known as one of the South's more select and genteel resorts with Beachy head on the southwest and the Downs behind it. It was even promoted by doctors as being invigorating to the weak and a sustaining tonic to the strong. It was 66 miles from London and the regular hourly service took 85 minutes from Victoria at this time. It had its own municipal orchestra (the largest in the Country) which played in the Winter Garden and a Grand Parade Bandstand which cost the princely sum of £40,000 in 1935. Famous military bands and well known concert parties played in the season.

However, Eastbourne not only sought to attract holidaymakers but also commuters to London. There were several electric expresses daily to London with Pullman Breakfast Cars. They even issued a booklet called 'Southern Homes on the Conqueror's Coast served by Southern Electric' in 1935 (see page 40) which advertised itself as a homeseeker's guide. The *Daily Press* wrote, at the time, 'So far as the expectation of life in general is concerned, it is better to live in the Country than in the town, and in the South rather than the North'.

The potential commuter was encouraged to visit the district before making his choice.

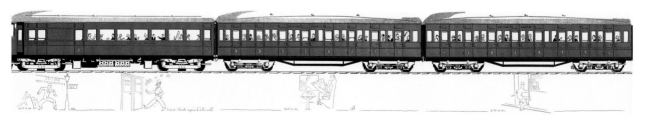

Seaford by Leslie Carr, 1930.
Seaford had a reputation for being a healthy resort favoured by people wanting a restorative holiday. It shunned the masses by not providing piers, concert parties, funfairs and other frivolities in favour of its natural charm.

Surrounded by the Downs to the north and east and the Seven Sisters Cliffs it was a sun trap and wind shielded. A booklet produced by the SR at this time claimed that: 'Seaford is most excellent for children; for anaemia, debility, convalescence; for tuberculosis, chronic bronchitis and catarrh'.

Have a Day Off on the Electric Coast
This unusual fold out leaflet was produced in 1935 to promote day travel to the seaside between Worthing and Hastings. The idea proposed was that instead of going to work it would be more fun to have a day by the seaside.

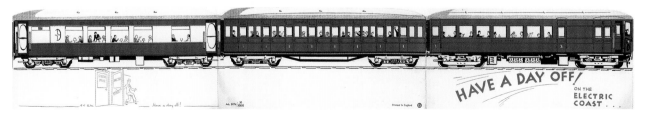

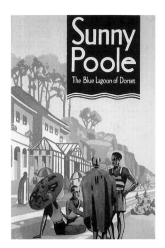

The 1934 Poole leaflet (above) extols the lovely harbour and pine clad shore while the 1940 wartime leaflet for Southsea (centre) explains that 'for sheer, downright enjoyment a holiday at Southsea, in spite of wartime conditions, could hardly be surpassed'.

The neighbouring naval city of Portsmouth gets a mention – and a jolly sailor – in this Southsea leaflet from the 1930s.

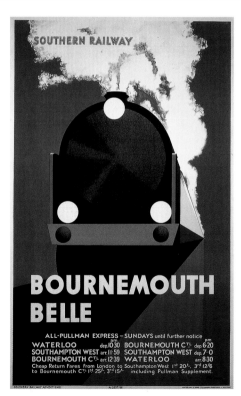

Bournemouth Limited

The Bournemouth Limited, the 2-hour non-stop express, commenced daily running on July 8 1929. It left Bournemouth at 08.40, returning from Waterloo at 16.30.

Bournemouth Belle

The Bournemouth Belle was introduced at the start of the summer timetable on Sunday July 5 1931. The Belle left London at 10.30 calling at Southampton at 11.59 and arriving at Bournemouth at 12.39. The return journey left Bournemouth at 17.10 and called at Southampton at 17.40 arriving at Waterloo at 19.18. The poster illustrated advertises the winter Belle that ran on Sundays only. From the start of 1936 the Belle became a daily service.

The 1938 Evenings by the Sea leaflet uses a two pronged approach. Either travel to the sea after work, hop on a train in London and you will quickly be in Brighton. Better still, live in Brighton and commute.

Not wishing any opportunity for publicity to be missed the Southern Railway produced a range of advertising bookmatches. Three are illustrated advertising the continuing success of electrification and the refreshment rooms at Waterloo Station run on behalf of the Southern Railway by Frederick Hotels.

Ramsgate by Kenneth Shoesmith and V. L. Danvers, 1939

Ramsgate 'on the Sunshine Coast' was famous for its boating and yachting. It was the first and most convenient harbour for boats proceeding down the channel from either the Thames or the East Coast ports. Ramsgate week, the regatta, always attracted a large gathering of racing yachts and onlookers and special railway excursion trips were arranged.

Unusually, this poster was produced jointly by two artists.

Broadstairs – Sea, Sands, Sunshine by John Mace, 1929.
Broadstairs was popular for day and weekend excursions because of its proximity to London. The South Eastern and Chatham Railway first advertised Broadstairs as a watering place and described it as 'The Children's Elysium' with firm sands and a splendid Sea View. The name is said to come from the width of the passage opening to the sea.

Folkestone by V. L. Danvers, 1947.
Although Folkestone was an important Roman and Viking settlement it was the construction of the South Eastern Railway in 1844 that brought it to prominence.

This poster was inviting a return to the holiday habit because most of the Southern Coastal resorts were effectively closed down during the Second World War due to the threat of invasion.

Hints for Holidays

Holiday travel was a very important part of the Southern Railway's activities. Nowadays it is hard to believe that during the life of the Southern Railway most holiday travel was undertaken by train. *Hints for Holidays* was the Southern Railway guide book giving details of resorts that could be reached by the Southern Railway. A large amount of information was included. As well as details of each town or area's facilities and how to reach the area by train more than half the book was taken up by advertisements for hotels and boarding houses.

The Southern Railway published *Hints for Holidays* annually each spring with the exception of the years 1941 to 1946 inclusive at a price of 6d. Each year saw the size increase with the 1930s editions running to 900 pages. Surprisingly a 1940 edition was produced albeit only about half the size of previous year's. Copies of this edition were also distributed during 1946 with an addendum slip. A new edition published for the 1947 season was the last produced by the Southern Railway.

Though all three constituent companies produced holiday guides the Southern Railway book takes its style from the London and South Western Railway guide book first published in 1899.

In 1926 the distribution, despite the general strike in May, was 100,000. The following page totals show the remarkable growth of this publication from 1924, the first year in which it included all three sections of the Southern Railway: 1924, 260 pages; 1925, 336 pages; 1926, 400 pages; 1927, 624 pages.

1927   1928   1929

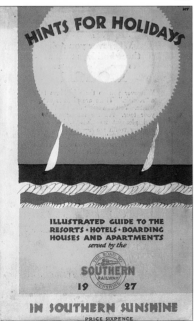

Overleaf: Covers for 1932 to 1940, top to bottom, left to right

HINTS FOR HOLIDAYS

PROFUSELY ILLUSTRATED.
LISTS OF HOTELS & APARTMENTS.
SOUTHERN RAILWAY 6D

HINTS FOR HOLIDAYS

PROFUSELY ILLUSTRATED.
LISTS OF HOTELS & APARTMENTS.
SOUTHERN RAILWAY 6D

HINTS FOR HOLIDAYS

Where to go
Where to stay

THE SUNSHINE GUIDE

6D

SOUTHERN RAILWAY

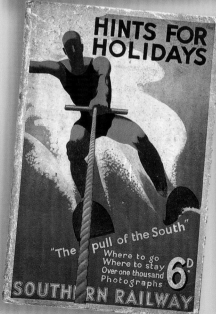

HINTS FOR HOLIDAYS

"The pull of the South"
Where to go
Where to stay
Over one thousand
Photographs
6D

SOUTHERN RAILWAY

HINTS FOR HOLIDAYS

Where to go
Where to stay
Over one thousand
Photographs
6D

SOUTHERN RAILWAY

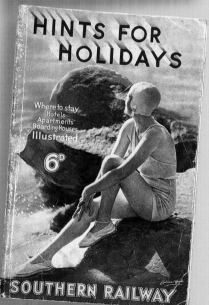

HINTS FOR HOLIDAYS

Where to stay
Hotels
Apartments
Boarding Houses
Illustrated
6D

SOUTHERN RAILWAY

Hints for Holidays 1947
The post war edition of this guide was somewhat smaller than the previous 1940 edition. The Southern Railway produced this edition in the hope that by now the citizens of Southern England were ready and waiting to go on holiday. Though with fewer pages than previously the guide still contains the same mix of advertisements and information. Also included were some full colour pages.

Camping

Like the other companies the Southern Railway provided Camping Coaches at many of its wayside stations in the holiday areas of Devon, Cornwall and the New Forest. The coaches provided were extensively adapted to contain all the holidaymaker could require. Looking through the list today it compares very favourably with a present day caravan right down to the corkscrew and bed linen.

Even though in its camping coach leaflets the Southern Railway was not very complimentary about the 'old way' of camping out, it was still very happy to provide leaflets for the holidaymaker with details of the camping sites in Southern England and how to get to them.

Rambles

Rambles books were produced, each covering a different part of the Southern Railway area. Walking was a popular pastime and the books provided detailed instructions for a number of walks in each area. The start and end point of each walk was normally a Southern Railway station. The Southern Railway provided tickets to allow outward and return journeys from the different stations.

The pre-grouping companies had produced rambling books and initially the Southern Railway carried on their offerings.

Southern Rambles for Londoners

This was probably the most popular book produced by the Southern Railway. Five very similar editions were published between 1931 and 1938. It contains details of 20 rambles in the London Suburban area served by the Southern Railway.

Walking at Week-ends

One edition, published in 1936, covered the area about an hour or two from London, including Canterbury and the New Forest. It contained 14 walks.

Walks in North Devon

Ten walks in North Devon are included in this 1928 book. All are from the route of the Atlantic Coast Express.

Let's Get Out Here

26 walks from the route of the Atlantic Coast Express are described in this 1937 book.

Hike for Health, *c.* 1930 (*facing page*).

The thirties were halcyon days for the Southern. The nation had recovered from the First World War unsuspecting of any further disruption. Apart from the usual summer rush to the sea and special summer events such as the Aldershot Tattoo, Rugby Union matches and Cowes Regatta there were the Sunday Ramblers' Excursions taking hundreds of enthusiastic walkers to some wayside station to enjoy the country air. The love of vast open spaces, fresh air and picturesque scenic views, away from the hustle and bustle of city life was an irresistible temptation.

HIKE for HEALTH
SOUTHERN RAILWAY
Go-as-you-please cheap tickets get you to the country quickest

Ask for details at any S·R Office and buy "Southern Rambles" by S·P·B·Mais 6 D

SOUTHERN RAILWAY ADVERTISING

THE
SOUTHERN RAILWAY
BRINGS THE COUNTRYSIDE NEARER

This is the exact size of the original miniature painting by Lt.Col. F.A.Goddard O.B.E. R.M.S.

'GO AS YOU PLEASE'
CHEAP DAY TICKETS
FROM LONDON
Tuesdays, Wednesdays & Thursdays by all trains except between 4·30pm & 6·30pm Please ask for folder at any London Station
FREQUENT TRAINS
QUICK TRAVEL

The Southern Railway Brings the Countryside Nearer, by Lt Col. F. A. Goddard, 1947.
The message here is that this happy scene can be yours for the price of a day return 'Go as you please' ticket. The ticket meant that ramblers and hikers could return home from a different station. Thus you could travel from London to, say, East Grinstead and walk from there to Horsham (with your dog) and return from Horsham. The only stipulation was that you returned on the same day.

Don't Miss Autumn in the Country
by E.E. Wise, 1934
The poster's contemporary rambling guide also listed things to beware of:

'Setting fire to dry bracken or gorse; trampling growing corn or long grass; leaving gates open; disturbing breeding pheasants; picking mushrooms; picking wild flowers indiscriminately or of uprooting any. You are not a locust. Leave the countryside at least as beautiful as you find it.'

Make the Most of the Autumn Days before the Leaves Fall by F.H. Coventry, 1939.
This poster was an attempt to encourage 'outings' by parties. Camping parties, sports teams and tours were encouraged to travel with cheap tickets and free reservations.

Winter Sunshine Holidays in Southern England

To complement the summer *Hints for Holidays* guidebook, the Southern Railway produced a companion edition for winter holidays. When first produced in 1925 it was titled *Winter Holidays in Southern England*. From the 1930 edition onwards the word Sunshine was included in the title, the Southern Railway presumably deciding that this would increase the number of people taking advantage of the facilities offered!

WINTER SUNSHINE HOLIDAYS

IN SOUTHERN ENGLAND
SOUTHERN RAILWAY

'Winter Sunshine' was strongly promoted by the Southern Railway. Londoners were encouraged to leave the City and enjoy the surrounding countryside. They were tempted with idyllic country scenes – and cheap tickets. Sample booklet covers are shown here and on the following two pages.

WINTER SUNSHINE

HOLIDAYS

in SOUTHERN ENGLAND

SOUTHERN

TICKETS

7-day **Season**

10/6 3rd Class

to see the District

The Cheapest Way

15/- 1st Class

RAILWAY

WINTER SUNSHINE HOLIDAYS —

—in SOUTHERN ENGLAND

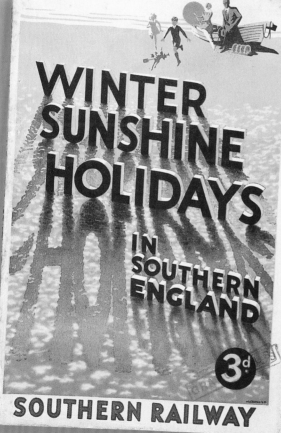

WINTER
SUNSHINE
HOLIDAYS

IN
SOUTHERN
ENGLAND

3d.

SOUTHERN RAILWAY

WINTER
SUNSHINE
HOLIDAYS

IN SOUTHERN ENGLAND

SOUTHERN RAILWAY

SOUTHERN RAILWAY

THIRD CLASS 10/6 ADULTS

7-DAY season tickets

TRAVEL WHEN, WHERE, AND AS OFTEN AS YOU LIKE

THIRD CLASS 5/3 CHILDREN (UNDER 14)

Winter Sunshine, 1935.
Winter walks were promoted by the Southern Railway in posters like this one. An organised party of eight or more going out for the day could travel at a single fare for a double journey. Books to accompany these trips were also available. In 'Southern Rambles for Londoners' by S. P. B. Mais [price sixpence] there were examples of 15-mile walks and a 'help' list. This suggested what the rambler should wear, what to do if lost and what to see. It also gave some interesting advice about the weather:

'The official weather forecast is seldom correct. The unofficial weather forecast of the postman or farmer is equally unreliable. The English weather defies all prophecy'.

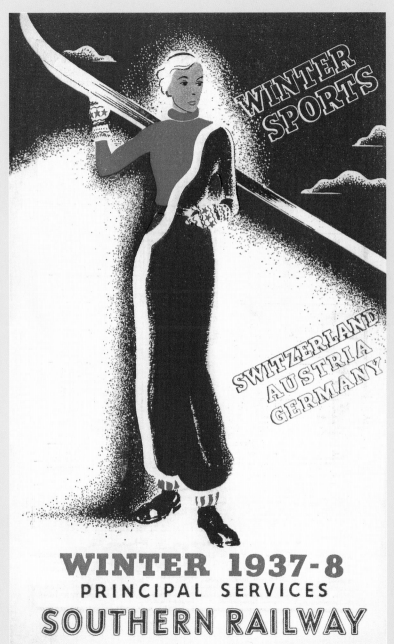

WINTER 1937-8
PRINCIPAL SERVICES
SOUTHERN RAILWAY

Winter Sports.
For the more ambitious (and well off) there were services to skiing and other winter sports on the Continent. The cover of this leaflet looks like that of a holiday brochure but inside it contained simple Continental timetables. It includes the resorts of Interlaken and Zermatt. Interlaken could be reached from London each day on the Oberland Express in just 20 hours.

ATLANTIC COAST EXPRESS

	5th JULY to 27th SEPTEMBER 1936				
	MONDAYS to FRIDAYS A.M.	SATURDAYS A.M.	SATURDAYS A.M.	A.M.	SUNDAYS A.M.
WATERLOO	10.35	10.35	10.45	11.0	10.50
EXETER CENTRAL	P.M. 1.42	P.M. 1.42	P.M. 2.2	P.M. 2.12	P.M. 2.4
ILFRACOMBE	3.32	3.32	–	–	4.4
BUDE	3.33	–	–	4.12	–
PADSTOW	4.31	–	4.57	–	–

SHEP

SOUTHERN RAILWAY

Atlantic Coast Express by Shep (Charles Shepherd)

On July 19 1926 the first 'Atlantic Coast Express' left Waterloo for its journey to North Cornwall. This train became the most multi-portioned train to run on the Southern Railway with through coaches to numerous destinations in Devon and Cornwall. Such was the popularity that relief trains were often needed as was required on the first days when the Ilfracombe-bound coaches ran as a separate train a few minutes behind the North Cornwall service.

The ACE appears on most advertising for the West Country though only one publicity booklet was produced about the train which describes what can be seen out of the window on the journey. The two walks books 'Let's Get Out Here' and 'Walks in North Devon' illustrated on page 22 both describe walks from the route of the ACE.

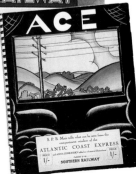

SEVERIN
DEVON BELLE
The DEVON BELLE
Fridays, Saturdays, Sundays and Mondays in each direction
dep 12.0 noon | Waterloo | arr 5.20 p.m
arr 3.16 p.m | Sidmouth Jct. | dep 2.3 p.m
arr 3.36 p.m | Exeter Ctl. | dep 1.40 p.m
arr 5.32 p.m | Ilfracombe | dep 12. 0 noon
arr 5.36 p.m | Plymouth Friary | dep 11.30 a.m
NEW!
ALL-PULLMAN TRAIN TO THE WEST OF ENGLAND
with Observation Car
SOUTHERN RAILWAY & PULLMAN CAR COMPANY

The Devon Belle by Marc Severin, 1947.
The introduction of the all-Pullman 'Devon Belle' in 1947 added yet another name to the list of famous British expresses. It brought a new standard of luxury to the journey westward and the added bonus of a specially constructed observation car. It ran from Waterloo to Ilfracombe. At the time it was referred to as 'The Glasshouse' and 'Britain's Only American style observation car'.

The Isle of Wight

Though the Isle of Wight is a small part of the area served by the Southern Railway a large amount of Isle of Wight publicity was produced. The fact that a journey by ship was required added to the holiday atmosphere. The Southern Railway owned and operated the ships and so there was even more information for its publicity to contain.

The whole range of publicity could be found for the Isle of Wight. Booklets giving details of hotels, boarding houses and features of each area of the Island complemented attractive small leaflets giving the briefest details. The Isle of Wight section of the 'Hints For Holidays' guide book was produced for many years as a separate booklet. Rail travel was actively promoted with leaflets giving details of weekly rover tickets.

To help pass the time on the journey to Portsmouth the Southern Railway produced 'The Passing Scene' giving information to the traveller about what could be seen from the window of the train from London.

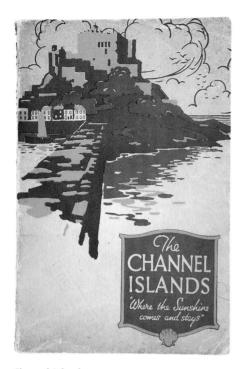

Channel Islands

The Channel Islands featured in holiday based publicity throughout the Southern Railway years. It was the one area in the UK where the usual rivalry between the Southern Railway and Great Western Railway was put on hold and joint publicity was produced, including the booklet shown above. This was produced in 1927 in two versions, one for each company, both using the same cover. The companies' ships used Southampton and Weymouth with passengers allowed to use either company's ship for return travel.

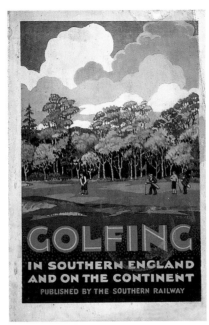

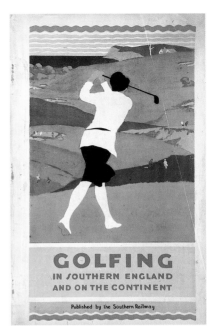

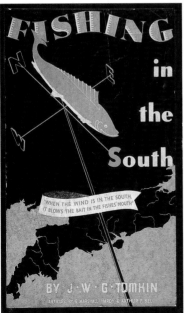

Sport

Not wishing to let any opportunity for leisure travel be missed the Southern Railway targeted publicity very strongly at those who played golf or went fishing. Golf books had been produced by the pre-grouping companies and were continued by the Southern.

Each year, well into the 1930s, guides were produced listing golf courses on the Southern Railway giving quite detailed descriptions of the courses, local area, nearby hotels, nearest station, fees, costs etc. An introduction written by a golfing expert, often the editor of *Golfing*, extolled the virtues of playing golf in Southern England. Much was made of the fact that by the early 1930s three out of four major golfing events were played on the links on the Southern Line.

The books did not restrict their attention to the UK. Lists of courses on the Continent were also included along with details of how to reach the areas by Southern Railway.

The other field of sport that was given a book of its own was fishing. *Fishing in the South* contained three articles on coarse, fly and sea fishing written by experts of the day. The rest of the book listed all the rivers of Southern England and how they could be reached by Southern Railway, where to buy fishing licences and in some cases nearby hotels and tackle shops.

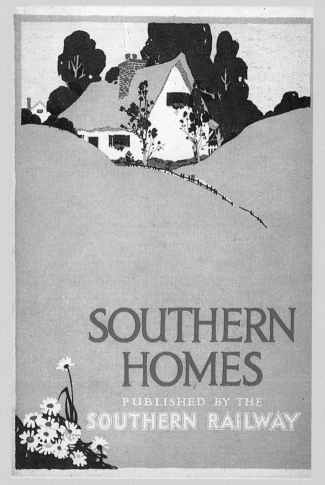

Southern Homes

The idea of persuading people to move out of London to the suburbs to attain a better quality of life was started by the London and South Western Railway well before the Southern Railway came into existence. The Southern Railway continued this idea with books extolling the virtues of the areas around London accessible by its trains. The books contained details and photographs as well as advertisements from Estate Agents inviting readers to rent or buy the new property in the area.

Electrification of parts of the Southern Railway produced a string of these books. For each new stage of the electrification plan a new book was produced to advertise the area which could now be quickly and easily reached by the new trains.

The first book covers all the area served by the Southern Electric and was produced to coincide with the new services to Brighton and West Worthing on January 1 1933.

As with most other SR booklets and publicity items, the cover artist is generally anonymous, but Horace Taylor managed to have his initials on the right-hand booklet on the facing page.

Southern Homes – Surrey and Hampshire
Published to coincide with the Portsmouth Direct electrification on July 4 1937, the area of Hampshire covered is restricted to the electrified Portsmouth and Alton lines.

Southern Homes – Sussex
Whilst covering the whole of Sussex this book was published soon after services started on the newly electrified line to Portsmouth via Horsham on July 3 1938. This included Chichester and Littlehampton.

Southern Homes for City Men
This book covered towns on the London to Brighton and Brighton to West Worthing lines and is unusual in that it preceded electrification by over a year. The intention of the book is clearly to get across the message that when the Brighton line is electrified property prices will rise and the reader should, therefore, buy now.

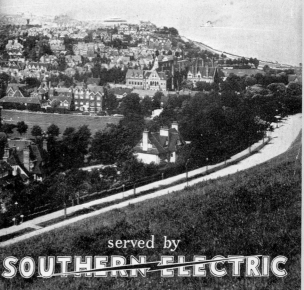

Southern Homes – Kent
This edition is unusual in that it does not seem to have been published to coincide with any newly electrified lines.

Southern Homes on the Conqueror's Coast
This book was published to coincide with the electrification of the East Sussex and Hastings area on July 7 1935.

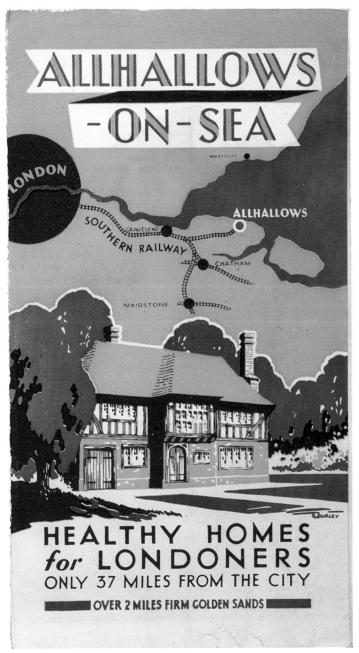

Allhallows-on-Sea was an area where 'healthy homes' were available. As in other areas electrification provided a major advertising opportunity.

Main Line Electrification

The *Southern Railway Magazine* announced the first phase of main line electrification thus: 'Sunday, July 17, witnessed the inauguration of the first stage of a further great Extension of the Southern Railway Electrification. This stage comprises lines from Purley to Three Bridges, also Reigate, and is part of the great Electric Extension scheme which will include the lines between London and Brighton and Worthing, and form the first main line electrification scheme to be undertaken in this country.'

It was the Government's decision to remove the duty it had imposed on rail fares that financed the main line electrification to Brighton. Companies were allowed to use the value of the duty on new schemes as a way of reducing unemployment.

Southern Electric

With each new phase of electrification new timetables had to be produced for the modified services. Prior to the new services appearing in the Southern Railway timetable small booklets were produced. The six shown here were produced to advertise the new electric systems completed between 1933 and 1939.

Party Travel

The London & South Western Railway produced books containing locations for 'Picnic and Pleasure Parties' in the early 1920s with the Southern Railway continuing the theme with its own publication. All kinds of parties were catered for with booklets produced to assist party organisers in finding the correct location for their day out. The traveller was given numerous options, including a trip to Portsmouth Dockyard, a coach tour of North Devon or even a trip to the Isle of Wight by air from Shoreham Airport. The leaflet cover below is one of the earliest while those on the right date from the 1930s.

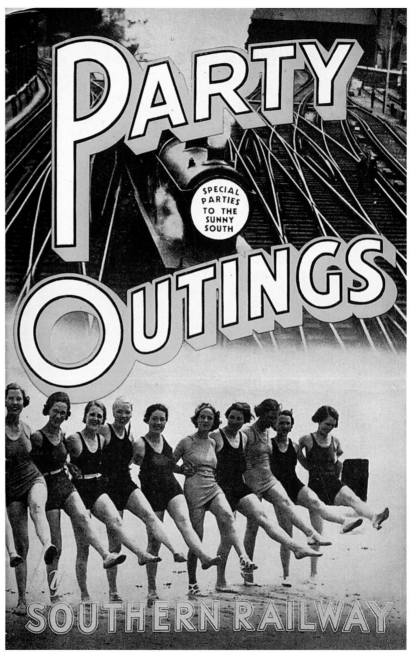

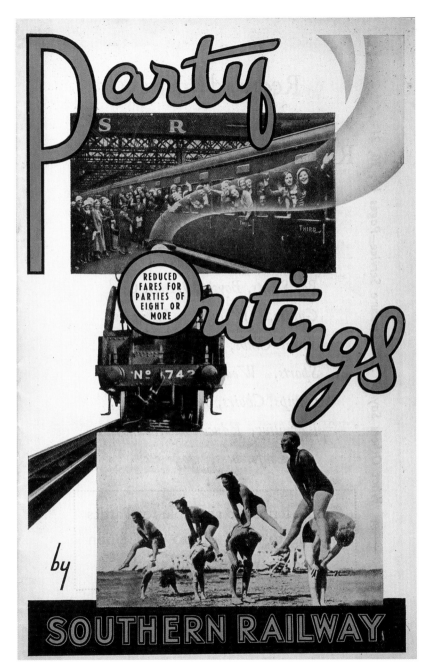

Party Outings

S R

REDUCED FARES FOR PARTIES OF EIGHT OR MORE

N° 1742

by

SOUTHERN RAILWAY

PARTY OUTINGS

PARTIES OF
8 OR MORE
SINGLE FARE
DOUBLE JOURNEY
EXPRESS TRAINS
CARRIAGES
RESERVED

SOUTHERN RAILWAY

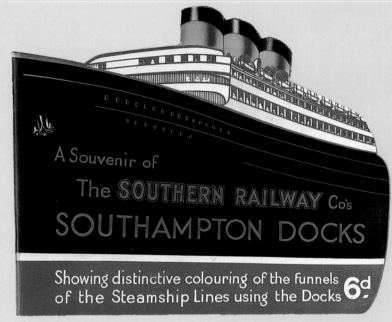

Southampton Docks

Southampton Docks appears in a vast array of publicity. As well as generating income from the actual movement of goods and passengers through the docks the Southern Railway created revenue from other sources.

When the big liners were in the Docks special trips were arranged for the public to 'see the liners', inclusive tickets being available for travel and entry to the docks. A number of guide books were produced for visitors giving, mainly, information about the shipping companies. The most attractive is *A Souvenir of Southampton Docks* produced in the shape of a liner.

The publicity was not directed solely at the UK population. Books were produced in French to inform those across the Channel of the facilities available.

The large area of land which was reclaimed to build the New Docks was used to provide what were called Factory Sites. Attractive publicity tried to persuade businesses to move to the area given the good transport connections.

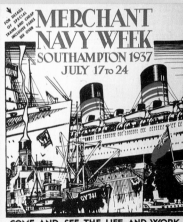

La voie d'accès en
GRANDE-BRETAGNE

C'EST LA LIGNE DE LA COMPAGNIE DU
SOUTHERN RAILWAY
D'ANGLETERRE

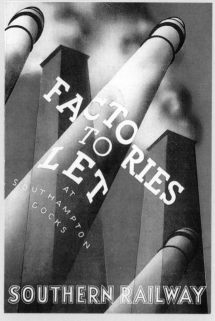

FACTORIES TO LET AT SOUTHAMPTON DOCKS

SOUTHERN RAILWAY

FACTORY SITES

AT SOUTHAMPTON DOCKS
SOUTHERN RAILWAY

Travel to England

The London and South Western Railway had realised the need to provide publicity to persuade travellers from abroad to visit Southern England. The Southern Railway continued to provide publicity targeted at two main areas: North America and France.

For the American market much was made of 'Visits to the Old Country' giving the impression that many who read the publicity were descended from the Pilgrim Fathers and would want to visit their homeland. The booklets strongly featured historical connections with Saxon and Roman England in the guise of Alfred the Great and Caesar. The French were provided with guide books in French very much on the lines of the English versions.

Waddington's produced playing cards for the Southern Railway (illustrated on facing page). Two very similar sets were produced, one showing a Southern Electric train and the other (illustrated) a ship. How the cards were distributed is not known, though the shipping cards may have been available on the cross-Channel ferries. Given that other publicity items were charged for it seems likely that the cards were also sold rather than distributed free of charge.

SAXON ENGLAND

With the Compliments of the
SOUTHERN RAILWAY OF ENGLAND

SR

EASY-
TOUR
TICKETS
from

ANYWHERE TO ANYWHERE IN SOUTHERN ENGLAND

PLEASURE TRIPS
SIGHT SEEING TOURS
BUSINESS JOURNEYS

SOUTHERN
RAILWAY

Outre-manche
et ses plages
et Londres aussi.....

HT

Edité par
le SOUTHERN RAILWAY
d'Angleterre

ENGLAND
... and why

Continental Travel – Getting There

All the Continental guidebooks contained information on travelling to the area. To supplement these the Southern Railway produced a wide selection of publicity covering just the travel aspect.

The earliest shown, the 1925 *'King Arthur to the Continent'* is a simple description of the route from London to the Channel port. Later these booklets contained detailed information on visas, foreign currency, passports etc and how to go about obtaining the items required. *'Let's Go Abroad, It's So Easy'* was available after the Second World War. Unfortunately by then many of the travel arrangements described were either discontinued or seriously reduced.

Travel abroad by car was becoming popular so leaflets on cross channel car ferries were produced in the later 1930s.

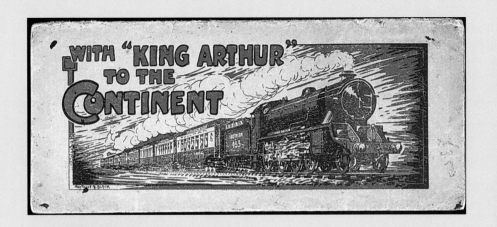

With "KING ARTHUR" TO THE CONTINENT

ENGLAND AND THE CONTINENT BY SHORT SEA ROUTES 1933.

SOUTHERN RAILWAY

EXCURSIONS TO THE CONTINENT AND CHANNEL ISLES SUMMER 1931

and until further notice.

SOUTHERN RAILWAY

For Through Bookings from G.W.R. and L.N.E.R. Stations see pages 29-32.

May. 15th, 1931.

Let's go abroad It's so easy!

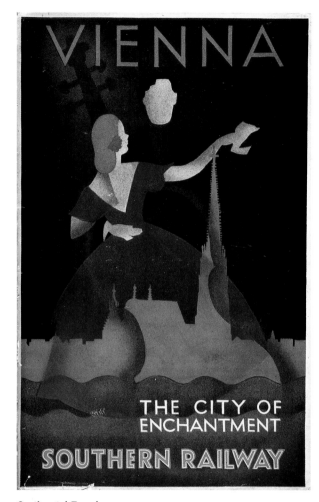

Continental Travel

The Southern Railway operated ships over many routes to the Continent. It was, therefore, keen to make available much information to assist the foreign traveller in choosing where to spend a holiday. The Southern Railway produced a series of guide books for all main areas that could reasonably be served by connecting services from the Channel ports. As well as the short sea routes between Dover, Folkestone and Calais and Boulogne its ships served Rotterdam from Gravesend, Dieppe from Newhaven, Le Havre and St Malo from Southampton and the Channel Islands from Weymouth. The Vienna and Belgium booklets above were published in 1936 and 1930 respectively. The 'Off the Beaten Track' series of small pocket size booklets was introduced in the first year of Southern Railway's existence and continued until the start of the BR regime in 1948.

SOUTHERN RAILWAY

AUSTRIA
ITS
Lakes and Alps
OFF THE BEATEN TRACK NO 21

'TWEEN
FLORENCE AND
ROME

OFF THE BEATEN TRACK NO. 22
SOUTHERN RAILWAY

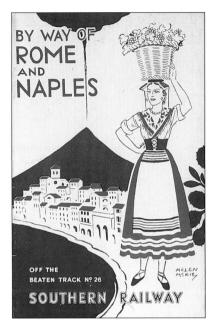

BY WAY OF
ROME
AND
NAPLES

OFF THE
BEATEN TRACK Nº 26
SOUTHERN RAILWAY

HELEN McKIE

SOUTHERN RAILWAY

THE LAND
OF THE DONS
OFF THE BEATEN TRACK ! NO. 8

SOUTHERN RAILWAY

THE
ITALIAN LAKES
OFF THE BEATEN TRACK ! NO. 17

ITALIAN
LAKES

OFF THE BEATEN TRACK Nº 17
SOUTHERN RAILWAY

The Southern Railway's 'Peerless Riviera' included both the French and Italian Riviera as well as the Rhone Valley, Corsica, Rome, Malta and Brioni Islands (now part of Croatia). *Peerless Riviera* was a new book produced by the Southern Railway; none of the pre-grouping companies produced a similar title. Southern Railway publicity advertised it as being provided to cater for 'the ever increasing number of English people who migrate annually to the Sunny South'. 'Rome, Cannes, Nice, Monte Carlo, sunshine and holiday, the Riviera waits, a brief twenty-four hours from London.' Richard Viner wrote the final edition, produced in 1931 with a cover by Horace Taylor (left), which included drawings by Helen McKie such as the one below. This was a new initiative, as previous guidebooks of this type had no reference to who wrote them. The higher profile for this title was, perhaps, not after all considered worth while as no further editions were produced.

NAPLES RIVIERA
SICILY & TRIPOLI

OFF THE BEATEN TRACK NO. 3
SOUTHERN RAILWAY

THE
SUMMER=TIME
RIVIERA
FRANCE & ITALY

G.S.B

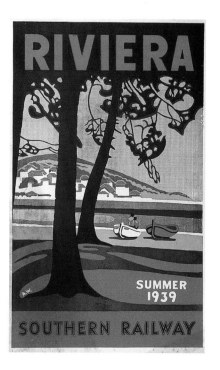

Through the four seasons of the year the sun shines. Winter sunshine, Spring sunshine, Summer sunshine, Autumn sunshine. It is the sun that tinges most faithful

Sunshine all the Year.

description of the Riviera with a glittering extravagance, but if, once again, it is suspect of too generous embroidery, let there come further and final endorsement to its pretensions in the hard test of approval. And the answer to that test is that for over a hundred years people have been going to the Riviera for its winter sunshine.

London (Victoria) – Paris

The main Southern Railway Continental service was to Paris. Twelve direct services left London throughout the day with the most famous being the 11.00 departure from Victoria, the all Pullman Golden Arrow. Such was the importance of the route that three further services contained Pullman cars. Journey times were about 7 hours with the Golden Arrow taking just 6 hours 35 minutes.

Most London to Paris travel was routed via Dover to Calais. Folkestone to Boulogne was also used as was one overnight service from Waterloo via Southampton and Le Harve.

Like other railway companies the Southern Railway owned hotels throughout the area it served. At Southampton the South Western Hotel overlooked the docks as did the London and Paris Hotel in Newhaven. London was also catered for with station hotels, one being the SR-owned Charing Cross Hotel from which the luggage label below originates. The hotel adjoined the station with direct access from the platforms.

PICARDY and PARIS
Published by the Southern Railway of England
PRICE SIXPENCE

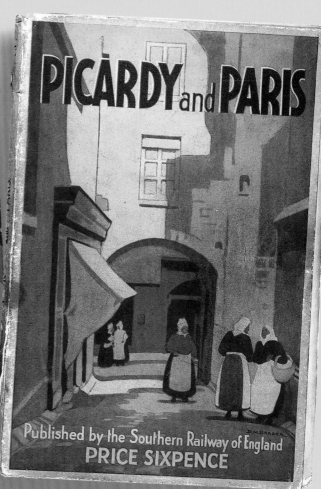

PICARDY and PARIS
Published by the Southern Railway of England
PRICE SIXPENCE

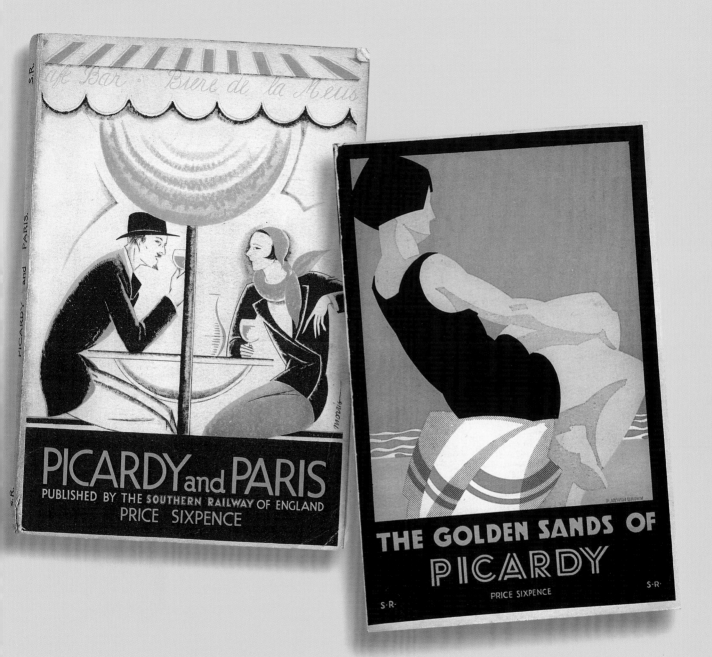

London (Waterloo) – Caen (for Normandy)

Advertised as the route to Normandy, Caen was reached by ship from Southampton, the connecting trains running from Waterloo, leaving during the evening. Outward journeys ran on Monday, Wednesday, Friday, with returns on Saturday, Tuesday and Thursday. Journey time was approximately 12–15 hours depending on the actual departure time from Waterloo.

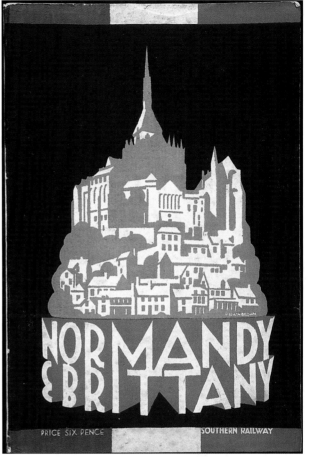

EXAMINATION OF BAGGAGE. The French Customs authorities are not unduly strict and are usually satisfied with a negative answer to their question. Passengers arriving in France, however, must be prepared to make a declaration of the contents of their baggage and personal belongings.

It should be noted that the following articles are liable to Customs duty:—Jewellery, new clothing, colonial products, alcoholic drinks, sets of pharmaceutical preparations for personal use, and, in a general manner, all new articles.

Matches, playing cards, foreign copper coins, medicines not included in an official pharmacopœia, drugs, and unauthorised editions of books are strictly prohibited.

On condition that a declaration is made, a passenger may bring with him, without payment of duty, twenty cigarettes, ten cigars or 40 grammes ($1\frac{3}{8}$ ozs.) of tobacco for consumption during the journey, but these quantities are not cumulative. The allowance of twenty cigarettes is also granted to ladies, but not to children.

Further Afield

The Southern Railway did not feel constrained to restrict its advertising to the UK or near Continent. The *Off The Beaten Track* series of booklets advertised such destinations as Egypt, Majorca, Dalmatia, Bavaria, Palestine and Hungary as well as countries nearer to home.

The journey to Palestine, which would today take a few hours by air, was enthusiastically advertised as follows. *It is an easy journey to Palestine. After leaving London (Victoria Station), you can get right through from Calais to Syria by train, the only needful change being involved in the crossing of the Bosphorus by Ferry at Istanbul. Leaving London on Friday Tripoli is reached on the Wednesday following.*

The 1935 booklet about Majorca gives a somewhat different image of the holiday location than is seen today. *There is no question about it, the first impression you get when you get to Majorca is the sensationally mediaeval appearance and manner of the local inhabitants. Spain is supposed to be two hundred years behind the rest of the world – Majorca is at least five hundred years behind Spain. The peasants look as purely Gothic as does their cathedral in Palma.*

SOUTHERN RAILWAY

EGYPT and SUDAN

OFF THE BEATEN TRACK! NO 15

MAJORCA

OFF THE BEATEN TRACK NO. 14.

SOUTHERN RAILWAY

ALONG THE RHONE VALLEY

OFF THE BEATEN TRACK NO. 7

SOUTHERN RAILWAY

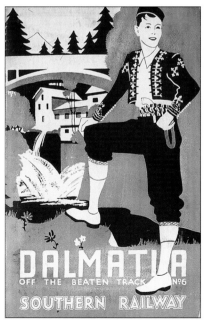

DALMATIA

OFF THE BEATEN TRACK Nº6

SOUTHERN RAILWAY

PALESTINE

OFF THE BEATEN TRACK! NO.19

SOUTHERN RAILWAY

HUNGARY

THE LAND OF THE MAGYARS

OFF THE BEATEN TRACK NO. 23

SOUTHERN RAILWAY

To provide the summer holidaymaker with information to plan the rail journey to his holiday destination the Southern Railway provided booklets covering the reduced fares available and the trains which could be used. The restrictions were often to particular trains on a particular day of the week. Return was expected a week or fortnight later. Over the August Bank Holiday weekend some flexibility was shown with return allowed on any of a number of days.

Unfinished leaflet
This leaflet was being produced by Helen McKie for the Southern Railway. Why it was never completed is not known.